Liberals at the Border:
We Stand on Guard for Whom?

The Honourable Lloyd Axworthy

Liberals at the Border: We Stand on Guard for Whom?

LLOYD AXWORTHY

Published in association with
Victoria University by
University of Toronto Press

© University of Toronto Press Incorporated 2004
Toronto Buffalo London
Printed in Canada

Reprinted 2004

ISBN 8020-8593-8

Printed on acid-free paper

The Senator Keith Davey Lectures

National Library of Canada Cataloguing in Publication

Axworthy, Lloyd, 1939–
Liberals at the border : we stand on guard for whom? / Lloyd Axworthy.

(The Senator Keith Davey lectures)
ISBN 0-8020-8593-8

1. Liberalism – Canada.   2. Canada – Foreign relations – 1945–.
3. Canada – Foreign relations – United States.   4. United States –
Foreign relations – Canada.   I. Title.   II. Series: Senator Keith Davey
lecture series.

FC635.A98 2004   971.064'8   C2003-902019-3
F1034.2.A93 2004

University of Toronto Press acknowledges the financial assistance to
its publishing program of the Canada Council for the Arts and the
Ontario Arts Council.

University of Toronto Press acknowledges the financial support for
its publishing activities of the Government of Canada through the
Book Publishing Industry Development Program (BPIDP).

Contents

BIOGRAPHICAL NOTES

Preface

On 11 March 2002 the Honourable Lloyd Axworthy delivered the sixth annual Senator Keith Davey Lecture in the Isabel Bader Theatre at Victoria University in the University of Toronto. Previous lectures, listed at the end of this publication, took place on the premises of our neighbour, the Faculty of Music. It was a particular pleasure to welcome Senator and Mrs Davey, and also the chancellors of our two universities, Kenneth Taylor of Victoria University and the Honourable Henry N.R. Jackman of the University of Toronto – both Victoria College graduates. The presence was noted of two other graduates of Victoria, David Clark, chair of the Board of Regents of Victoria University, and Wendy Cecil, chair of the Governing Council of the University of Toronto. Ms Cecil brought greetings on behalf of U of T and its president, Robert Birgeneau, whom we also warmly welcomed.

Following Ms Cecil's remarks, Madame Justice Rosalie Abella introduced the speaker. The occasion was brought to a close with comments by the speaker's brother, Dr Tom Axworthy.

The themes of national sovereignty and identity discussed so knowledgeably and persuasively in this lecture are of perennial interest, but they have taken on a particular urgency for Canada in recent times. Victoria University is grateful to Dorothy Davey for her assistance and advice; to the many friends and colleagues of Senator Davey whose support has made this annual lecture series possible; and above all to the Honourable Lloyd Axworthy for this articulate defence of liberal values, ideals, and practices.

Paul W. Gooch
President
Victoria University
in the University of Toronto

Opening Remarks

Introduction

MADAME JUSTICE ROSALIE SILBERMAN ABELLA

I want first to thank President Gooch and especially the incredible political juggernaut that is Keith and Dorothy Davey, two of Canada's most cherished treasures, for the privilege of participating in this wonderful lecture series.

Everyone knows about Lloyd Axworthy's indispensable role in banning land mines, in introducing the concept of human security to the international community, in leading the ban on child soldiers, and in promoting the International Criminal Court. For these and other humanitarian interventions, he has received honorary degrees, the Order of Manitoba, the 2001 World Peace Award, and a nomination for the Nobel Peace Prize. He even made a list by George

Veczey in the *New York Times* a couple of weeks ago as one of the sixty best things about Canada. So the interesting question is not what Lloyd Axworthy has done, but why he has done it.

Ever since he got his PhD at Princeton in 1972, through his many cabinet positions in the federal government, and even now as head of the Liu Centre for the Study of Global Issues at the University of British Columbia – where his life now includes some of the trappings of normality, such as time to be with his remarkable wife, Denise Ommanney, their wonderful son, Stephen, and their new granddaughter – he has used his humanitarian ideas to provoke the complacent into moving the world away from how it is and closer to how it should be.

And that is why Lloyd Axworthy is the ultimate public servant. His life's mission has been to eliminate barriers to Canadian citizens' opportunities to lead a qualitatively enhanced life at home and a morally enhanced one on the international stage.

This after all is a man whose core values were forged intellectually and spiritually in the smouldering afterglow of the International Declaration of Human Rights (1948), which committed a chastened world to the elimination of intolerance. The collective indignation that inspired the declaration lit a fire under Lloyd Axworthy that has never gone out. His brilliance enabled him to grasp how the integrated force of history, economics, politics, and human nature shapes the public interest; his energetic enthusiasm permitted him to devote the relentless hours it takes to try to change the world; his wisdom allowed him to build the personal and institutional links that transformed his beliefs into results; and his compassion helped him to understand that focusing public policy on those people in the world who have less is the better policy path even for those who have more.

Lloyd Axworthy has spent almost his entire life in government because it above all sets the stage on which the public gets to act out its aspirations. Because he was committed to helping as many people as possible achieve as wide a range of aspirations as possible, Lloyd committed himself in government to giving citizens the props that they needed to turn themselves and their country into the best that they could be.

As you would expect of someone in the business of changing the world, Lloyd has generated his share of controversy. Not everyone felt that the status quo needed renovating, and many inhospitable states were irritated by his allergic reaction to their injustices. Lloyd duly noted these criticisms, duly analysed them, and duly ignored them. He knew that delivering justice meant sometimes passing through some unfriendly neighbourhoods, but that never scared or deterred him from what he saw as his unwavering duty, nationally and internationally, to make fairness available to the greatest number. On the contrary, his record of public service is a record of escalating chutzpah and, as a result, the record of a public servant who never lost his relevance.

Lloyd Axworthy is not a man of his times, he is a man who helped make them. It is an honour to introduce to you a visionary intellectual, a passionate humanitarian, a magnificent husband and father, and a man I am proud to be able to call a friend: Professor Doctor Minister The Honourable Lloyd Axworthy.

The Sixth Annual
Senator Keith Davey Lecture

Liberals at the Border: We Stand on Guard for Whom?

THE HONOURABLE LLOYD AXWORTHY

Six months ago today, terrorists attacked the World Trade Center in New York and the Pentagon, near Washington, DC. Shock waves from that assault are still reverberating in most corners of the world. The hijacked planes turned into fiery projectiles by a fanatic's creed destroyed more than precious lives and collapsed more than structures made of concrete and steel. They shook the foundations of many hallowed beliefs, undermined accepted wisdoms, and shattered accustomed ways of thinking and acting.

Canadians responded to the tragedy of our southern neighbours with sympathy and understanding. We shared their deep revulsion at the remorseless killing of innocent people, and our government has shown unequivocal support for U.S. retaliatory actions. Our national agenda has become consumed with preoccupations of border management and anti-terrorist measures that serve to demonstrate solidarity in the war against the new barbarians.

Increasingly, however, the immediate and necessary responses to 11 September have been swept along in a whirlwind of decisions and a cascade of military and diplomatic initiatives by the United States that substantially change the global landscape. Security has become the all-powerful mantra, driving out most other concerns. The declared war on terrorism obscures the deadly toll of a half-million casualties a year, mainly civilians, in civil conflicts. Prospects of expanded military action threaten division in the global community. Force, not resolution, is too often the arbiter of disputes.

Eight months before the terrorist attack, the coming to power of a new U.S. president changed the political coordinates in Washington from centre to right. The advisers to President Bush – old pros from previous Republican administrations have seized on the call to arms against terrorism as a chance to assert an agenda that sees the world organized around an American hub, based on U.S. military dominance, with the United States showing little regard for international treaties, agreements, or institutions. At first, after 11 September, it seemed that coalition-based collaboration might prevail, but the signs of that grow dim. The current buzz word in Washington is 'maximum spectrum dominance.' Just a trifle chilling, if you think about it!

This double-punch combination of a breach in continental security and a U.S. administration steeped in aggressive unilateralism creates a major headache for Canada. Managing the relationship was challenging enough when the Clinton White House offered broad support for international architecture. It is far more daunting when the executive mansion is occupied by a wrecking crew dedicated to dismantling that architecture, riding the wave of a crusade against an 'axis of evil.'

Pierre Teilhard de Chardin, the Jesuit theologian, has written 'There are a great many portents, political and social upheavals, religious unease that have caused us all to feel that something tremendous is taking place in the world. But what is it?' That is a question that many people now ask – or at least should ask. A half-year after that stunning event of 11 September, the time has come to take stock. We should look hard at what has transpired. We should consider whether the unfolding trend of events is to our liking, suits our values, or represents the kind of choices that we should be making, given the special political, economic, social, and cultural DNA that Canadians have ' bred in the bone,' to use Robertson Davies's felicitous and unscientific phrase.

In response to the turmoil and in unease, the question 'What is it?' – along with its follow-up 'What do we do about it?' – animates this year's rendition of the Davey Lecture.

I thank the Board of Regents of Victoria University and Dorothy Davey for the invitation to join this distinguished gathering. It gives me an opportunity to pay personal homage to a man who in no small way shaped my own entry into and apprenticeship in politics and who, during his remarkable public career, gave its current shape to one of the enduring anchors of Canadian political life – the Liberal Party. We in this country are not very good at acknowledging our political builders and engineers, almost embarrassed to admit that they exist. So I welcome this chance to say 'Thanks' to the Senator.

And I can think of no more fitting and appropriate way for us, in his presence, to show our appreciation than to engage in an open discussion and public debate about the defining decisions facing Canadian liberals, especially those of the large-L Liberal variety, as this country stands on the border of an important fault line in our national life.

It may seem a little inappropriate, in these hallowed academic halls to concentrate on what might appear a partisan subject. And I must confess that even after a year of strenuous efforts by my academic colleagues at the University of British Columbia to rehabilitate me from my past pursuits, I can't help reverting to form, especially in the company of so many former partners in crime. But there is more to this exercise than old habits reasserting themselves. There is an undeniable reason for looking at where liberals stand: where they stand will determine in no small measure what decisions will occur.

In that respect, we should take lessons from Senator Davey. No one relished more the practice and pragmatics of party politics. As longtime director of the party, he was truly a happy warrior in mastering the intricacies of democratic electoral politics. But always for a reason. For Keith the game had a goal – it was the promotion of Canada.

He has always been passionate about this country and a great believer in its destiny. And no one believes more fervently in the crucial role of democratic party politics – in his case, Liberal Party politics – in defining, through open and active debate, a role for Canada. The party was not just a machine, but a forum where differences were heard and agreements hammered out.

The Canadian–U.S. Border and Why It Matters

A Recurrent Theme

My brother Tom and I were reminiscing a few weeks ago about the time in the mid-1960s – with me just back from graduate school and Tom an undergraduate at United College in Winnipeg – when we were visited by the Senator, known then as 'the Rainmaker.' Unusual for someone from Toronto to seek out western Liberals, especially snot-nosed, wet-behind-the-ears western Liberals. At a time when Walter Gordon and Mitchell Sharp led differing forces in the party over foreign ownership – then the defining issue of our relations with the United States – he appealed to us to become engaged in the unfolding debate.

We did. And we will never forget the packed ballroom of Ottawa's Chateau Laurier Hotel, with long lines of party heavyweights, masses of the rank and file, and young Liberals behind the mikes debating long into the night. We knew instinctively that something momentous was taking place, that this was one more station on the road to economic integration that was being fought out by the party. Note that it was the party that had the debate.

The same crossroads was met in 1988 when another generation of Liberals had to decide on the crucial issue of free trade. Once again we faced a hard choice – between the economic realities of increasing cross-border trade and all its benefits and the nagging sense that each step down the path of integration would diminish our freedom to choose and our range of manoeuvre. The early 1990s brought a renewal of the same issue as we wrestled with the Tory legacy of the NAFTA agreement.

Plus ça change, plus c'est la même chose.

The border has thus been a defining issue for Liberals as long as I can remember, and, through them, a defining issue for the country. Always in play was the difficult calculation of how to derive the benefits of sharing North America with one of the world's powerhouses, yet managing to maintain and defend political and economic space that we could call our own.

It was never an easy balancing act, but one that a majority of Liberals over the years saw as worth doing. Lester Pearson's stand against the Vietnam war, Pierre Trudeau's mission against nuclear arms, John Turner's campaign against free trade, and Jean Chretien's opening to Cuba – all illustrations of how different Liberal leaders at different times gave Canada a distinctive voice.

A few years back, while visiting President Leonid Kuchma of Ukraine, I asked how Canada could help his nation in its newfound independence. He said, 'Send me someone who can tell us how to live next door to a giant without being eaten.' This capacity to keep out of the clutches of a 500-pound gorilla was in his eyes a distinctly Canadian skill.

Is it still? Would the same question be asked today? Since 11 September new realities have been altering our position, so that even if it were asked we might now have a hard time answering. U.S. backlash in response to security leaks, potentially leading to hiccups and official U.S. harassment at the border, has created nervousness in boardrooms and around cabinet tables, underlining the tough truth that our continental interdependence is not cost-free.

We all know the profound impact that integration has had on our economic life. The latest sign: recent takeovers by American firms in vital sectors such as oil and gas and finance are raising fears of a 'hollowing out' in our business centres across the land. The latest panacea is a common currency. These raise difficult issues that must be faced.

Now, as well, a security blanket imposes a whole new set of demands for compliance and accommodation. Changes to refugee and immigration law, severe limitations of rights in our justice system, a push to make us more integrated in military matters, and the muting of any comments that the U.S. administration might construe as criticism reflect our new political correctness.

Some observers have argued that this approach is tactical and for the short term – simply a realization that the time calls for prudence and probity. But if each tactical step results in a further reduction of Canadians' capacity to exercise their freedom of choice, then we have given away too much latitude, compromised too many positions. We may find ourselves someday like a Newfoundland lobster, boiled to death by degrees.

As the rest of this first part of my lecture shows, U.S. pressure on Canada in matters of continental security has increased dramatically since 11 September, and other countries are watching our responses as possible guides to their own actions. The lecture then turns to four possible elements in Canada's long-term approach to global security – multilateralism, looking to Mexico within the North American framework, developing our own made-in-Canada strategies, and acting as a global catalyst for change.

Continental Security since 11 September

The security issue has given added zeal to those in this country who have long lamented that Canada wasn't nearly as compliant to the dictates of Senator

Jesse Helms or the Pentagon as they believe any right thinking country should be. They play the 'don't poke them in the eye' game, which means, for example, don't stand up for Canadian business when extraterritorial legislation prevents trade. Or don't sponsor a land-mines treaty or an international court because the U.S. generals don't like it. Or don't push for a plan to limit the use of child soldiers, or call for a nuclear review in the North Atlantic Treaty Organization, or defend human rights at the United Nations, or expand our peacekeeping, peace-building capacity because it doesn't fit with the anti-internationalist stance of the present U.S. administration. These Canadians have become the J. Alfred Prufrocks of this country, who ask, 'Do I dare to eat a peach? Do I dare disturb the universe?' if some American in high office objects.

Unfortunately the right in Canada has seized on the security issue to assert its own ideological agenda and too often goes unchallenged by Liberals — in some extreme cases, even has its positions adopted by Liberals.

Let me point to two recent initiatives, the first involving Afghanistan and the second, continental security. Canada sent troops to Afghanistan to be part of U.S. units mopping up the caves, searching for Osama bin Laden, and securing Kandahar's airport. There is nothing intrinsically wrong in our being part of a military effort to destroy the al-Qaeda network; our troops are acquitting themselves in good professional fashion.

But an imbroglio ensued when we found out that Canadian commitments to international law were not shared by the Americans. We had to engage in fancy footwork to explain away, if we ever did, our complicity. This situation should give pause to all those who believe that robust action as part of an American force should be our way of the future.

What I regret is the opportunity that Canada lost to burnish its standing as peacemakers working under UN mandate to help in the restoration of peace, order, and good government for the people of Afghanistan.

I was in the region in November, visiting the camps, talking to Afghan volunteers, trying to arouse support to counter the human tragedy that was taking place. I heard a heartfelt cry for help – not for more combat soldiers, but for builders and peacekeepers. Canada could have taken a lead in helping to define the nature and role of an international presence, used its scarce resources not as fungible for U.S. military capacity, of which there is more than enough, but to be a major player in postwar reconstruction in a country that today is verging on anarchy.

This was another opportunity lost to exercise a peace-making vocation long cherished by Canadians, but one that we seem increasingly reluctant to fulfil. At a recent meeting that I attended, a veteran Canadian public servant, now holding an international position, lamented that we no longer are seen as being engaged with the UN on vital issues of nation-building – our ranking as a peacekeeper is now number twenty-four. We are remitting our international political currency.

The second alarm involves negotiations on Canada's joining a new U.S. command for 'heartland defence' in North America. In my mind this is one of the most crucial decisions that Canadians of this era will make, with far-reaching consequences for future generations. Bland assurances have been issued that this is nothing to get excited about. Why shouldn't we integrate? ask some; after all, there is a threat to North America, and we should all do our part.

I readily agree that we should do our part – but at what price, for what reason, and in what way?

Before Canada proceeds too far down this road, we must ask – and answer – some important questions. Let's start by determining if the threat of terrorism is best met through military means, behind a fortress wall? Or is it better addressed by creating on the world stage a global network to supply intelligence, police power, and detection of threat at source and by having a wide variety of nations work with non-governmental organizations and private corporations to mitigate the terrorist threat?

In 1997, I first raised the issue of global terrorism at the meeting of the Human Rights Commission of the UN, pointing out that it represented a prime criminal threat to the security of individuals and would require substantial multilateral cooperation and real resources. We had some success in getting international treaties passed. But we could never enlist broad-based interest and had trouble getting ratification of these principles in Canada. In fact, the 'don't poke them in the eye' school of thought in Canada derided these efforts, saying that human security – the threat to individuals – was not a problem. The idea of centring protection on people rather than on nations, of focusing the international system on criminal threats rather than on military aggression, of working towards multilateral co-operation rather than relying on individual national defence, did not fit their worldview of Realpolitik.

Michael Howard, the Oxford historian, has written in the journal *Foreign Affairs*: 'To use or misuse the term war is not simply a matter of legality or pedantic semantics. It has deeper and more dangerous consequences,' creating a war psychosis that may be totally counterproductive, arousing immediate expectations and demand for spectacular military action. 'The use of force is seen no longer as a last resort, to be avoided if humanly possible, but as the first resort and the sooner the better.' Shouldn't we at least return to the concept of terrorism being a criminal act and apply the tools of criminal justice on a worldwide basis to restrain and control it, instead of retreating into a fortress?

Consider as well possible complications from a merger of Canada's armed forces under U.S. command for our various international undertakings to which the United States has not subscribed – bans on land mines and child soldiers, Geneva conventions, the International Criminal Court. We have been a leader in forging international laws that hold nations and individuals accountable under law. How do we create a unified Canadian–U.S. command with different troops following different rules? What do we do about the protocols to the Geneva convention that limit use of certain weapons? Canada has signed them; the United States has not. Under unified command, whose rules prevail? What does a Canadian soldier do if asked to handle land mines on Canadian soil in contravention of treaty undertakings? What if Canadians apprehend someone considered a war criminal under the soon-to-be-established International Criminal Court. U.S. law would prevent Canadians from turning over that person to the world body, despite Canadian obligations. Do you really think the Americans have the patience for a dual system?

To deepen the quagmire, a joint command could foreclose future policy choices for Canada. What can we say other than 'Ready, aye ready' on missile-defence schemes if we are part of an integrated system of homeland security. And if we can't say 'No' to missile defence, can we say 'No' the next step – a space-based weapons system. As the *Globe and Mail* recently revealed, Canada's military planners are already working in close cooperation with their U.S. counterparts on military space research, even though it potentially contradicts our stated policy and consumes substantial resources that might better go to equipping our troops for mobile peace-making missions And if we can't say 'No' to these cherished U.S. ambitions, then do we simply abdicate a role or responsibility to pursue effective arms-control architecture?

What is our position in defending and promoting an international, Canadian-made regime for the Arctic under a North American homeland command? The United States doesn't accept our sovereignty in that region or the need for any form of international rule-making. It has strategic interests there, so its attitude is 'Rules be damned.' It's pretty hard for us to assert our rights if we are in the same ship or under a U.S. commander. So, as melting of the ice and the impact of climate change transform our northern environment, we are in danger of relinquishing the ability and foregoing the responsibility to shape its future and determine its potential. Surely our northern peoples need to be involved in any decisions?

Let me put this question to you. Why would we transfer the use of force – the central ingredient in a nation's capability to protect itself – to another state, especially to one that by its own admission doesn't wish to abide by the same rules of international law and conduct that we believe are essential for an orderly world? In the past we have delegated certain sovereign rights under multilateral auspices to the UN or NATO for peacekeeping or humanitarian purposes; we do so with the right to participate fully in shared decision making. Why delegate such rights to another country that explicitly doesn't agree to delegate any of its own authority or to give much space for others to decide? Put it to the test: ask the United States if it is prepared, under the proposed new homeland command, to accept a rotating head commander, with equal turns between Canadian and

American generals. You and I know what the answer would be.

It is time to wake up and recognize that each step towards further alignment, integration, and acquiescence, each in its own way perhaps arguably appropriate, may just be the step that makes us the continent's permanent deputy sheriff. That is the Rubicon by which we now stand.

The World Is Watching

As important as it is to us, such integration has import and meaning for the broader international community as well. What we do in carving out a separate (if connected) trajectory vis-à-vis our powerful neighbour may affect many other countries. In 1969 Pierre Trudeau likened our position next to the United States to sleeping in the same bed with an elephant – you have to be careful it doesn't roll over on top of you. Many other nations are now in the same relationship. Strange as it may seem, all the world is now like Canada, wrestling with U.S. dominance. As President Kuchma's request showed, many countries see our intricate system of treaties, cross-border institutions, good relations, and innumerable private transactions as a model for how to share a common space with a powerful neighbour. Now,

since 11 September, and in the present U.S. hege-
monic mood, how we continue creatively to maintain close ties, yet retain our freedom of action, can
be a template for others to emulate. We are on the
front line. If we can't keep our identity while living
in proximity to a great power, then many other states
will suffer the same fate.

Canada and Global Security

Multilateralism

The biggest mistake we can make in this pathfinder
role is to become too fixated on, too preoccupied
with, too compliant and, too tied down in bilateral
dealings. Being one-dimensional and obsessed with
our southern border is a short-sighted prescription.
You simply can't deal one-on-one with a country that
powerful, tough, and aggressive and hope to escape
pressures to conform. Those people who counsel
such a course are leading us down the wrong path.

Instead, we should play to our strengths as an
active player in an increasingly crowded global village, which has become a swirling, proliferating con-
stellation of associations, networks, organizations,
and coalitions. A recent *Globe and Mail* story head-
lined 'Canada Jumps in Ranking on Globalization,'

detailed how this country has become one of the leaders in its adaptation to and aptitude for global activity, not just in economic terms, but in the range of political contacts and in the use of information technology. The authors of the study conclude that we are one of the nations best equipped to manoeuvre in global circles. Darrell Bricker and Edward Greenspon, in their latest book, *Searching for Certainty: Inside the New Canadian Mindset*, report on the increasing appetite and confidence that Canadians display in competing in the world – just ask our two Olympic hockey teams from 2002.

We should use our capacity as a joiner, convenor, builder, and implementer of multilateral, perhaps supranational bodies to exercise influence and set agendas. We ought to tap into the globalizing instincts of Canadians, their desire to 'move and shake' abroad, to establish presence and position. We can extend our appetite for being 'wired' into an international communication strategy. We should make the 'global village' (Marshall McLuhan's term) our turf. That is what the global index is telling us.

The surge of globalization has opened new avenues of endeavour. We see this in recent examples of Canadian leadership in the Commonwealth, the G-20, and the Organization of American States; we Canadians have helped create and organize new international institutions – the Arctic Council and the Human Security Network. We have a reputation of being honest and constructive, whether acting as government, as civil groups, or even as business organizations, despite one or two exceptions. The more we expand and enhance that role, the more we can operate according to the navigational guide of our own north star, not as a lesser light in a U.S. galaxy. The more we immerse ourselves in the work and activity of global networks, developing the social capital of the international system, the better our chances of keeping our actions distinctive and in accord with our own choices.

Sergio Marchi – a former colleague of mine and Liberal member of Parliament from this area until becoming Canada's ambassador to the World Trade Organization – made the case simply and clearly in a recent speech to the Canadian Club. 'In the end, the best way to achieve our nation's trade and economic goals is through multilateralism.' Amen. (I would add security and political goals.)

Looking to Mexico

Paradoxically one place to start is on our own continent. We need to articulate a broad concept of security that includes Mexico, establishes a transparent and functioning trilateral system of consultation and participation involving all three nations, and sees North America not as a fortress, but as a community.

A few years back, then U.S. Secretary of State Madeline Albright, Mexican Foreign Secretary Rosario Green, and I established a trilateral session of foreign ministers that met two or three times a year to look at a host of North American issues. One of the distinct advantages for Canada in a continental framework that includes Mexico lies in our having a partner in dealing with the colossus that sits between us. Canadian officials still find this new possibility hard to accept, nurturing anachronistic fondness for an alleged special relationship, so they have quietly dropped the trilateral approach.

Recently, former Mexican foreign minister Jorge Castaneda, writing on the 'op-ed' page of the *Globe and Mail*, indicated that Mexico has an interest equal to Canada's in maintaining good relations with the United States framed in terms of rules and institutions that offset peremptory demands from Washington and offer parity in decision making. If there is to be an active pursuit of security cooperation, we should resurrect the trilateral process and bring it into play.

In fact we could learn invaluable lessons from the Mexicans on how to enlist public and political support in the United States. It has over thirty consulates in that country, spread around regions, compared with our ten. These offices are able to network, make contact at the local level, tap into opinion, and solicit support. Getting Canadian officials outside the Washington beltway to cultivate an understanding and more knowledgeable U.S. public and to forge alliances with sympathetic Americans, whether on softwood lumber or UN peacekeeping, would constitute an essential task of public diplomacy. Just think of how successful Jamie Salé and David Pelletier were in Salt Lake City at righting the wrongs done by figure-skating judges. Maybe we need to have them give lessons to our foreign policy establishment.

More than process is involved. We need to develop good ideas to address serious security concerns within a North American framework, recognizing that the best defence is a good offence. During our trilateral meetings, three issues of common concern came to the table – transportation, energy, and water. Each in its own right could be the topic of a separate lecture. But let me give you the flavour.

First, transportation corridors: we discussed using the best green-and-blue technology combining major environmental and security techniques in a co-operative fashion. We looked at joint planning on upstream transit security in ports of origin, as an alternative to huge expenditures on border cops, as proposed by Canadian senators.

Second, energy is already a major security issue as a consequence of 11 September, and uncertainty in the Middle East. So far we in Canada have been basically reacting to Washington's initiatives. It announced a continental energy policy based on expanding supply; we responded by promising to expand production. But there is a complication, if not a contradiction here. We have also committed ourselves to reducing carbon emissions under the Kyoto agreement. So far the two goals don't mesh. There is an American-sponsored continental energy plan, but not a corresponding plan about climate change. Hence an emerging domestic dust-up because of the perceived disparities. One option is to bring the three countries together to discuss a cooperative strategy on melding energy and environmental plans in a sustainable way. A task force that I chaired for the Manitoba government recommended a North American emissions trading agreement that would provide a market mechanism to reduce costs. Simply put, the emitters pay for conservation efforts that reduce carbon emissions. It is but one idea that could form the basis of a North American strategy to meet international obligations.

Third, water looms large in the future of North

American security, both in its availability and in its management. Canada and the United Sates began pilot projects under the International Joint Commission for pre-emptive planning and effective cross-border procedures for making decisions on water. It is time to ask Mexico to join the IJC and to give it a mandate to begin creating a blueprint on water that preserves the right of each country to manage its resource, inside a mutually agreed system of management. We mustn't be afraid to tackle such issues, as long as they are in a serious, rule-making, trilateral framework. That is much better than being forced by U.S. congressional fiat, as we are already experiencing in the midwest cross-border watersheds.

Getting Our Act Together

These examples show three related but important aspects of the security debate – a broad definition of security, a clear plan, and adequate resources. First, the issue of security cannot be narrowly defined. It is not exclusively, or even primarily, a military imperative, nor should it be obsessively focused on the Canadian–U.S. border. We Canadians need to think creatively about how to rewire the institutional, treaty, and political circuitry into a North American context if we are to maintain our ability to exercise the right of decision making. The existing framework is antiquated and at times irrelevant. We can no longer rely on ad hoc, transactional diplomacy in Washington to protect our interests. It is an unequal contest. At the same time, buying in to a U.S.-dominated and -managed organization is exactly the wrong way to proceed. We need to propose a trilateral procedure that respects the autonomy of each partner as a way of addressing security issues.

Second, we have to get our domestic act together in Canada. This is not business as usual, as we have so clearly seen since 11 September. A great deal is at stake, and our national priorities need to centre on preserving our independence and promoting our global role. Ours should not be a defensive posture, but a proactive, made-in-Canada policy that enjoys the support and understanding of Canadians. To make this happen we need a maximum of openness and public debate, not decisions made behind closed doors. It should begin with the federal Liberal Party. With a convention in the offing, it is time for a serious review and debate à la Kingston, Peterborough, Harrison Springs – an opportunity to establish a distinctive Liberal take on a crucial issue facing the country.

Parliament must truly become the forum for the people in debating these issues. I applaud the deci-

sion to initiate reviews of foreign and defence policies (a similar review on economic integration would
be a nice complement). To make these reviews work
and give Parliament a voice requires a real effort by
the academies, the think tanks, the media, civil interest groups, and business leaders to look seriously at
new paradigms and propositions. It is time to get
away from old shibboleths and cranky characteriza-
tions of anti-Americanism or pro-continentalism.
We are handicapped and diminished by the paucity
of new ideas and dynamic intellectual reasoning.
Breaking out of the box, using brainpower to find
solutions, should be a Liberal priority.

Third, talk is cheap, unless there is a commitment
of significant resources to translate ideas into action.
There has already been a draw on the federal treasury
in Ottawa to beef up border control and to pay for
the military action in Afghanistan. These are immediate expedients. Are we also prepared to allocate
what is necessary to bolster foreign aid, particularly
to restore our international reputation as committed
and concerned people in the fight against disease and
the prevention of conflict? Let's retool defence expenditures to provide for mobility and surveillance
capacity and contribute to a UN rapid reaction force.
Expanding our diplomatic network both in North
America and around the world is essential to giving

effective presence and profile to Canadian issues and interests and to enhancing our global intelligence gathering. Developing transportation infrastructure as part of a North American network; investing in environmental technology, renewable energy resources, and conservation measures; planning for the protection and improvement of our water supply; and circulating an international information strategy are essential tasks in a broad-based program of human security. We must undertake and pay for such projects if Canadian leadership is to be taken seriously in the world.

In 1993, when the Chrétien government came to power in the midst of an economic crisis of confidence, the call was made for a national effort to restore our economic integrity. It worked, the country responded, and we fixed the problem. We need a similar call to action today to preserve our political integrity.

Catalysts for Change

That call to action goes to the heart of the special, distinctive contribution that Canada can make to the world's search for security. We must cast this quest as an indivisible and universal effort, a public good for all people, not just a pursuit of national security for a few select and exclusive groups or countries, based on an outmoded concept of sovereignty. Forty per cent of the victims in the World Trade Center were non-Americans from eighty countries, including Canada. The attackers were from a variety of nationalities united in their hatred of the values and principles of what they saw as a corrupt, secular, insensitive, and dominant ruling global system. They used the tools of modern finance, communication, and transportation to penetrate the defences of the strongest nation in the world. The risk that they represent cannot be met by one country or even by a coalition of countries acting alone or in isolation from the rest of the world. Everyone has a stake. Innocent people around the world are at risk from the dark underside of the global system, which fosters the growth of drug cartels, traffickers in humans, arms traders, and terrorists.

The eleventh of September brought North Americans face to face with this reality. In a sense we joined the rest of the world in recognizing our vulnerability. We now share the threats to the lives and livelihoods of ordinary people that have created a stalking, everyday fear for so many people around the world and it reminds us of our common humanity. We can see the breakdown of order in parts of the world; failures by marginal states to provide responsible government; gross violations of human rights; an increase in violence against individuals by governments, warlords, and criminals; and scarcities of public goods – the most important of which is security. We recognize that we cannot immunize ourselves from the impact and effect of these forces, and so we must come to understand that resistance requires a reordering of the global compact. We can no longer afford to say, 'We don't have a dog in that fight.'

Our vocation as Canadians should be to serve as catalysts for change in global practices and policies. Three very distinct global developments – involving international law, sovereignty, and Africa – bear strong traces of Canadian paternity. First, there is the imminent coming into force of the International Criminal Court (ICC), only five nations shy of attaining the sixty ratifications to trigger its establishment.* Here is the first new international institution of this new century, the cornerstone of a universal system of justice that will hold those who commit serious war crimes accountable and establish the base for a 'global rights revolution' to use the phrase of Michael Ignatieff, a previous Davey Lecturer.

Next month we celebrate the twentieth anniversary of Canada's Charter of Rights and Freedoms,

---

*The Statute of Rome entered into force on July 1, 2002.

one of the great contributions of liberalism to the defining of a Canadian culture of rights and tolerance. The Statute of Rome offers the same potential internationally. We can take the lead in asserting the rule of law over the rule of force. We played a major part in its creation of the ICC, and we must now make a similar effort for its implementation and in the campaign for its universal acceptance, even though there is opposition, notably from the present U.S. administration.

Second, running in parallel is the chance to transform the definition of sovereignty in order to enhance the worldwide protection of innocent people. After the mass murders, genocides, and ethnic cleansings that marked the end of the last century, and following the anguish and effort of trying to mount humanitarian interventions in the Balkans, Rwanda, East Timor, and elsewhere, a fundamental debate arose on when and where and by what means the international community can come to the aid of people under threat and override the rights of oppressors to hide behind a wall of sovereign jurisdiction.

In response to a call from Kofi Annan, UN secretary-general, Prime Minister Chrétien announced establishment of an International Commission on Intervention and State Sovereignty to initiate a global inquiry. In December 2001 the commission responded with a creative definition of sovereignty. It should not be the impregnable refuge of national interest, but rather 'the responsibility to protect.' To quote the report: 'The debate about intervention for human protection should focus not on the right to intervene but on the responsibility to protect.' Assessing who bears such a responsibility implies an evaluation of the issue from the perspective of the victim, not of the intervener. If a state cannot provide such protection or is the author of the crime, then it forfeits its sovereign right, and the international community steps in. The responsibility to protect means not just reacting, but also preventing and rebuilding.

The key is to have this new definition of responsibility properly debated and eventually confirmed by the UN General Assembly. It can lead to an effort to change the concept of state responsibility and the meaning of sovereignty. The United Nations could put in place a different norm and standard for judging state action and for combatting state terrorism, rooted in the universal right of security for the individual. What we began we should now complete and in so doing provide a value added to the makeover of the global system.

Third, an opportunity for us to propel this global liberal agenda, especially in Africa, occurs in June, when we host the G-8. Here is a chance to enlist the world's power elite in a serious examination of new ideas and new structures — not a customary practice for some, but one that could give this meeting substance and scope. The prime minister's initiative in putting Africa on the agenda has drawn attention to a continent that has been sorely afflicted by human insecurity and suffering because of disease, poverty, conflict, violence, crime, and terrorism. What better place is there to begin protecting people through prevention, reaction, and rebuilding, and to assert governments' responsibility to protect as the touchstone of a new global regime of justice and rights.

I can give you a clear example of what it would mean from my recent trip to northern Uganda, right on the border with Sudan. During the last fifteen years a vicious conflict has killed thousands of people and forced 400,000 others into squalid, disease-ridden security camps. Those who leave the camps to forage for firewood or water are in imminent jeopardy from land mines strewn about by the rebels and the army. Children are readily kidnapped and turned into child soldiers or, in the case of young girls, forced into years of sexual slavery. It is a forgotten part of the world and doesn't draw CNN to display its misery to the world. Yet the suffering and tragedy of its people are as great as the tragedy we witnessed on 11 September and deserve an equal response. There are real heroes at work in this region – NGOs and local aid workers. At a local hospital – started up three decades ago by a Canadian woman – I discovered that a year and a half ago such people became the firewall in stopping the spread of the virulent Ebola virus, brought to the area by the armies in the conflict. Twelve doctors and nurses died in a heroic action, not only saving the lives of thousands in the area, but also preventing the virus's potential escape into the wider global community. They didn't get their pictures on the cover of *Time* magazine, but in my view they deserve our heartfelt thanks. Their effort should be a wake-up call to the rest of us that we can do no less.

The narrative of politics is the human story, not the soliloquy of the state. This is a story that needs telling at the G-8.

Conclusion

I began by raising the question of what border Liberals should defend. Are we to become enmeshed in a complicated set of arrangements and entangling commitments as part of homeland security? Or is there an alternative, much more in keeping with our values, our talents, and our interests? I would say that there is another type of border where we can make a stand. This means not working for a world that divides itself into enclaves of privilege and power, where force and military dominance are the measures of who governs. It means choosing to work for a world based on the rule of law, with universal respect for human rights, where the responsibility to protect the innocent is a global standard.

This is not a trouble-free prescription. It means sticking one's neck out and expending political capital. It means expecting to fail at times and learning to accept frustration and disappointment. But it is a task that we can perform.

The question is: are we Canadians ready and willing to be at the centre of an international effort to revise the global system? This is a choice that can't be made in the backrooms or in cloistered diplomatic clubs. It would clearly be a turning point. It has to be the product of an open, transparent, democratic debate – the kind of exchange that Liberals held in the Château Laurier's ballroom four decades ago.

As a Canadian liberal, I fervently hope that, when and if such a self-examination takes place, we Canadians will emerge with this answer to the question of where we stand – saying to the rest of the world, particularly those who seek our help, people such as the children of Gulu in northern Uganda – 'We stand on guard for thee.'

Biographical Notes

The Honourable Lloyd Axworthy

Lloyd Axworthy graduated with a BA from United College (now the University of Winnipeg) in 1961, obtained his MA in political science from Princeton University in 1963, and earned a PhD from Princeton in 1972.

Lloyd Axworthy's political career spanned twenty-seven years – six years in the Manitoba legislative assembly and twenty-one in Parliament. Elected in 1979 as Liberal MP for Winnipeg–Fort Garry, he was re-elected in 1980, 1984, 1988, 1993, and 1997. He held several cabinet positions, notably at Employment and Immigration, Status of Women, Transport, Human Resources Development, Western Economic Diversification, and Foreign Affairs.

At Foreign Affairs, he became internationally known for his advancement of the human security concept, particularly the Ottawa Treaty - a landmark global treaty banning anti-personnel landmines. For his leadership on landmines, he was nominated for the Nobel Peace Prize. For his efforts in establishing the International Criminal Court and the protocol on child soldiers, he received the North–South Institute's Peace Award.

He continues to be involved in international matters, leading the Canadian delegation to The Hague Conference on Climate Change and chairing the advisory board of the International Commission on Intervention and State Sovereignty (ICISS).

Lloyd Axworthy is currently director and CEO of the Liu Institute for Global Issues at the University of British Columbia and holds positions on several boards and companies. He joined the law firm of Fraser, Milner, Casgrain as a consultant on trade and international affairs.

He is a board member of the MacArthur Foundation, Lester B. Pearson College, University of the Arctic, Impacs (Institute for Media, Policy and Civil Society), and the Conflict Analysis and Management Advisory Board at Royal Roads University. He is also chair of the Human Security Centre for the United

Nations University for Peace (UPEACE); co-chair of the State of the World Forum, Commission on Globalization; member of the Eminent Persons Group on Small Arms; and chair of the Manitoba Task Force on Climate Change. In July 2001, Dr Axworthy became a special representative for UNICEF Canada. He was Duke University's Karl von der Heyden Distinguished Visiting International Fellow for 2001.

Since leaving public life in the autumn of 2000, Dr Axworthy has been the recipient of several prestigious awards and honours. In 2002, the Vietnam Veterans of America Foundation presented him with the Senator Patrick J. Leahy Award in recognition of his leadership in the global effort to outlaw landmines and the use of children as soldiers and to bring war criminals to justice. In February 2002, Princeton University awarded him the Madison Medal for his record of outstanding public service. He received the CARE International Humanitarian Award and the Thakore award honouring the peace work of Mahatma Gandhi and was invested into the Order of Manitoba. In May 2002, he accepted an honorary doctorate from Dalhousie University to accompany previous honorary degrees from the University of Denver, Niagara University, the University of Victoria, and the University of Winnipeg.

Dr Axworthy lectures widely in Canada, the United States, and elsewhere. He is married to Denise Ommanney. They have three children: John, Louise, and Stephen. He makes his home on the west coast of Canada.

Senator Keith Davey

———————

Keith Davey was born in Toronto on 21 April 1926 (the same day as Queen Elizabeth), the son of Charles 'Scotty' Minto Davey and Grace Viola Curtis Davey. He attended North Toronto Collegiate Institute, graduating in 1946, and went on to Victoria University, where he received a BA in 1949. He was an excellent student and president of the Student Council, although in his typically self-deprecating fashion he recalls that at one point his grades were so poor he had to surrender the Senior Stick. His humility prevents him from noting that the prized honour was awarded to the student with the highest grades who also participated actively in campus life.

Following his graduation from university and a

Senator Keith Davey

brief stint at the Faculty of Law, he went to work for Foster Hewitt and CKFH radio station in sales, rapidly becoming sales manager – a position that he held for eleven years.

In 1960 he ventured into Canadian politics as Liberal campaign organizer for his home riding of Eglinton in Toronto. Having already served as president of the Toronto and York Young Liberal Association, he became national organizer of the Liberal Party in 1961. From 1962 to 1984 he was chair or co-chair of eight national Liberal election campaigns. *Globe and Mail* columnist Scott Young dubbed him 'The Rainmaker' in honour of his ability to precipitate votes for his favourite candidates. Senator Davey would later use this title for his political memoir, *The Rainmaker – A Passion for Politics*, published in 1986.

In 1966 Prime Minister Lester B. Pearson appointed him to the Senate. His various contributions there included chairing the important Senate Committee on Mass Media. He worked closely with Prime Ministers Lester Pearson and Pierre Trudeau, offering political advice and sharing warm and loyal friendships.

After he retired from the upper house in 1996, before the required age, his colleagues, led by Senator Jerry Grafstein, raised funds to honour his contribution to Canada and to its political life by establishing a lecture series in his honour at Victoria University. Though retired from the Senate, Keith Davey is still active in politics and as a family man, and he is an avid sports fan. He is married to Dorothy Elizabeth Speare, and they have three children – Catherine, Douglas, and Ian – eight grandchildren, and countless friends.

The Senator Keith Davey Lectures

John Kenneth Galbraith
The Socially Concerned Today
(University of Toronto Press, 1997)

Michael Ignatieff
'The Liberal Imagination: A Defence'
(January 1998)

Ruud Lubbers
*Revitalizing Liberal Values
in a Globalizing World*
(University of Toronto Press, 1999)

Lord Roy Jenkins
The British Liberal Tradition
(University of Toronto Press, 2001)

Madam Justice Louise Arbour
War Crimes and the Culture of Peace
(University of Toronto Press, 2002)

Lloyd Axworthy
*Liberals at the Border:
We Stand on Guard for Whom?*
(University of Toronto Press, 2004)